IN THIS SERIES

Auto Racing

Baseball

Basketball

Football

Golf

Hockey

Lacrosse

Soccer

Tennis

Track and Field

Wrestling

THE COMPOSITE GUIDE

to **AUTO RACING**

JOHN F. WUKOVITS

Sunnyside El.
Media Center

CHELSEA HOUSE PUBLISHERS
Philadelphia

Produced by Choptank Syndicate, Inc.

Editor and Picture Researcher: Norman L. Macht
Production Coordinator and Editorial Assistant: Mary E. Hull
Design and Production: Lisa Hochstein
Cover Illustrator: Cliff Spohn
Cover Design: Keith Trego
Art Direction: Sara Davis

First Printing

1 3 5 7 9 8 6 4 2

Library of Congress Cataloging-in-Publication Data

Wukovits, John F., 1944-
      The composite guide to auto racing / John F. Wukovits.
          p.   cm.—(The composite guide)
      Includes bibliographical references (p.) and index.
      Summary: Surveys the history of auto racing, from the early
beginnings to its status as America's most popular spectator sport.
      ISBN 0-7910-4722-9
      1. Automobile racing—History—Juvenile literature.
      2. Automobile racing drivers—Juvenile literature.
      [1. Automobile racing—History.] I. Title. II. Series.
GV1029.15.W85 1998
796.72—dc21   97-51901
                                                                    CIP
                                                                    AC

CONTENTS

MESHING THE HUMAN AND THE MECHANICAL

A hundred scattered thoughts swamped Mario Andretti's mind as the start of the 1969 Indianapolis 500 approached. Having qualified for the middle of the first row, Andretti found himself flanked by two other top drivers who, between them, had captured four previous Indianapolis trophies—the legendary A. J. Foyt with three victories, on his left, and the defending champion, Bobby Unser, on his right.

Though Andretti had driven in five earlier Indy 500s, he had yet to win. In each of the past three years, an unfortunate combination of bad luck and mechanical failures had slapped him in the face: an engine failure in 1966, a lost wheel in 1967, and a second engine failure in 1968. His car's sponsor, Andy Granatelli of the STP Oil Company, had financed cars at Indianapolis 16 times without winning

Andretti believed 1969 could be different. He drove a machine that he thought "would blow everything else off the tracks"—a turbo-charged Lotus. Some observers gushed that the bright red, wedged-shaped vehicle with the powerful engine would revolutionize the industry. Andretti said that driving the car "was like walking through the looking glass into the 21st century." He was so convinced of the Lotus's effectiveness that he mused, "If I was ever going to win the 500, it would be in this car."

However, the advanced technology came with a price. To give the car greater speed, the designer,

Mario Andretti celebrates his 1969 Indianapolis 500 victory in which he set a speed record of 160.218 mph. The trophy for the 53rd running of the race is behind him.

Colis Chapman, used lightweight materials for many parts. As a result, the Lotus carried a troubling reputation for losing wheels because one of the lightweight parts would snap. Chapman and the men who worked with him faced one of racing's universal quandaries. In attempting to push the machine to the limit and squeeze out as much speed as possible, they also placed the driver at the edge of safety. Somewhere a line existed beyond which the machine could not safely operate. It was their job, and Andretti's, to discover where that line rested.

Problems started to plague the Lotus during practice runs. The powerful turbine engine gulped gasoline like water, so a way had to be found to increase the miles per gallon without dropping the car's speed or general performance. Then, one week before the race, the right rear universal joint snapped and had to be replaced. Andretti and his pit crew—the men who slaved over the car, installed its parts, and tuned the engine to its maximum— figured that these were simply the normal pre-race wrinkles that needed to be ironed out. They understood that a man and his machine forged a finicky relationship that required constant care and attention.

On the day before qualifying for the race was to begin, Andretti took the Lotus out for a high-speed run. As he headed into one of the track's turns, he heard a "whirr-r-r" sound coming from the vehicle. "It's a sickening sound to a race driver," he recalled. "It means that something is coming off the machine."

The Lotus's rear end had collapsed, breaking the right wheel and sending the car into a maddening 320-foot spin. Debris and sparks flew in all directions as the Lotus smacked into the concrete wall, scraped along its side for 60 feet, then came to an abrupt stop in the middle of the track.

"I thank the dear Lord that I wasn't stunned by the impact," Andretti said later. "I covered my face with one hand and unsnapped the seat belt with the other. By this time I could feel the heat through my uniform. That wasn't too bad, but the heat around my face was almost unbearable."

An ambulance whisked Andretti to the field hospital, where physicians treated the racer for second degree burns to his upper lip, nose, and cheeks. Fortunately, he avoided other injuries and was quickly released. Though shaken by the experience, Andretti was eager to return to the track, for crashes and injuries were simply facets of racing that all drivers faced.

Mario Andretti is set to start the 1969 Grand Prix at Sebring, Florida, in his favorite Lotus.

When Andretti's pit crew inspected the damaged car, they discovered that a weakened hub, which no one had noticed during an inspection, had sheared off and sent the right wheel spinning and bouncing down the track. Andretti, who like other drivers depended upon and trusted the pit crew to maintain the vehicle in top form, was angry that the cracked hub had avoided notice. "That hub should never have been passed, and the oversight had nearly cost me my life."

His crew redeemed itself over the next 24 hours by working non-stop to ready Andretti's backup vehicle so he could take it out on the track the next day. Though he did not expect this second car to perform as well as his Lotus, Andretti qualified for the first row by reaching speeds of just under 170.

Excitement swept through the 350,000 spectators who packed the Indianapolis Motor Speedway to watch the 1969 race and built to a crescendo as Tony Hulman, president of the Indianapolis Motor Speedway, barked out his command, "Gentlemen, start your engines!" At that moment the first of 33 drivers zoomed across the starting line, including the 29-year-old Andretti and the other two members of row one, Foyt and Unser.

Though Andretti sped to an early lead, he did not intend to push his car to the limits and risk overheating. Instead, he wanted to see how the car performed, then plan the race according to its capabilities. He gradually built speed until his heat gauges started to rise, then adjusted the engine revolutions until he brought the gauge back to normal range. He decided that he could safely race the car at around 165 miles per hour, a speed that would place him ahead of most of the field. However, he knew that if Foyt's car ran smoothly, he could do nothing but hope for second place. Maybe luck, he mused, would finally be on his side.

But on the fifth lap, something ruptured and sprayed liquid into the cockpit. Since his oil and water temperature gauges shot up at the same time, Andretti thought an engine hose must have sprung a leak, requiring an unscheduled pit stop and precious minutes lost. After slowing down and watching Foyt grab the lead, Andretti located the source of the liquid. A plastic bottle of Gatorade that had been strapped into the cockpit had burst.

Though relieved, Andretti hesitated to place too much strain on his engine, so he eased off for a while. Roger McCluskey sped past him into second place, but Andretti was content to trail along for the next 40 laps, using only as much power as needed to stay in the other racers' shadows.

On the 51st lap Andretti pulled in for his first scheduled pit stop and watched helplessly as his crew, anxious to avoid spilling even a drop of the precious fuel, took longer than normal. By the time he rejoined the racers on the track, Andretti had fallen farther behind Foyt and McCluskey.

Foyt then experienced his own problems. On the 80th lap he pulled into the pit area so his crew could determine why his engine kept losing power. After 24 agonizing minutes, the pit crew located and repaired a tiny 10-cent metal clasp that had broken. But Foyt's chances for victory had disappeared.

Four-time winner A.J. Foyt passed a record 10,000 miles in his 29th Indy 500 in 1986.

McCluskey dropped from contention when he ran out of fuel. Though Andretti took the lead on lap 85, he lost it 19 laps later when once again his pit crew took too long to refuel. In the interim, driver Lloyd Ruby grabbed such a commanding lead that all he needed to do to capture the victory was make one normal pit stop and avoid any accidents.

This was to be Andretti's day, however. Ruby pulled into the pit area on lap 106. When a crew member signalled to Ruby that refueling had been completed, the racer started to pull away. Unfortunately, one of the refueling hoses had not yet been disconnected from his fuel tank, and when he sped forward the hose ripped out part of the tank. Ruby had no choice but to forlornly lift himself out and walk away from the dismantled vehicle.

Andretti now knew that if he avoided over-heating the engine, the race was his. Far ahead of the pack, he was able to ease off and drive at slightly slower speeds than normal. He barely averted tragedy on lap 150 when he momentarily lost his concentration and came perilously close to hitting the outside wall. He regained control a few feet from the wall.

The cagey Foyt, even though he trailed Andretti by many laps, tried to egg Andretti into racing him, but Andretti had nothing to gain by taking on Foyt one-on-one. Now was not the time to get involved in a meaningless, though exciting, driving contest.

When a victorious Andretti crossed the finish line with an average speed of almost 157 miles per hour, shattering the previous year's record pace by four miles, a beaming Andy Granatelli waited to give his driver a huge bear hug. Two men who, through a combination of ill luck and misfortune, had never captured the title now embraced as champions.

The race typified everything that made auto racing the exciting sport that it had become: the enormous amount of sweat and labor needed to prepare a car for racing, the always-present element of danger that threatens a racer's life, a driver pushing or pampering his machine so it works to its highest peak of efficiency, the reliance on the pit crew, and the knowledge that luck can negate every single precaution and the most skillful driving. This meshing of men and machines had all begun on a small track a little over 100 years ago.

2

"MAKE THEM ALL ALIKE"

Inventors had long been intrigued by the notion of a motorized vehicle. As far back as the 13th century, English scientist Roger Bacon wrote that "cars can be made so that without animals they will move with unbelievable rapidity." Two centuries later Italian genius Leonardo da Vinci sketched rough ideas of a mechanized military vehicle similar to a tank.

The first practical use of a motorized contraption occurred in 1769 when a French artillery officer, Nicholas Joseph Cugnot, constructed a three-wheeled carriage propelled by a steam engine. Though its top speed of three miles per hour hardly threatened the horse, it was nonetheless an initial step. A Belgian mechanic, Etienne Lenoir, successfully developed the first internal-combustion engine—powered by gasoline—in 1860, which German inventor Nicholas Otto improved in 1878.

The next step was to adapt engines so they could be used to move machines. Karl Benz of Germany added a motor to a tricycle in 1885; his fellow countryman Gottlieb Daimler hooked up motors to bicycles and boats. Daimler then created a more powerful engine by increasing the revolutions per minute from Otto's 200 to his own 900, to power a four-wheeled, gasoline-driven carriage. Emile Levassor of France produced another early version of an automobile in 1891 when he attached a motor to a buggy.

Developed by Francis and Stanley Freelan, the steam-powered auto known as the "Stanley Steamer" was popular before the rise of gasoline-powered engines. This photo, taken in the 1920s, shows an 1898 Stanley Steamer still in use.

This sudden rush of inventiveness caused an automobile boom in France between 1895 and 1908. Since the nation already boasted a superb road system, France dominated this early era in automobile design and production.

Meanwhile, similar events occurred in the United States, where a ready market existed for the automobile. The bicycling craze had swept across the country in the 1890s, casting thousands of people onto roads and giving them a taste of independent travel they had never known. The American public, though, wanted more powerful machines than the bicycle.

An enterprising individual needed little more than mechanical knowledge and a place to assemble his device to get started in the business. Scores of men disappeared into their garages to produce what they were sure would electrify the nation and make millions for themselves. However, intense competition and

The first mass-produced car in the United States was the Ford Model T. Henry Ford, the pioneer in assembly line car production, sits in a circa 1904 Model T with his son Edsel. The car was available only in black.

the uncertainty of what would appeal to the public caused most endeavors to quickly disappear. One early automaker, Charles Duryea, estimated that six out of every 10 companies went bankrupt between 1900 and 1908.

The survivors transformed the United States from a horse-and-buggy nation into a motorized country. On September 21, 1893, Charles and Frank Duryea opened the American automobile era by attaching a one-cylinder gasoline engine to a carriage. Three years later Henry Ford startled onlookers when he drove his quadricycle through the streets of Detroit, Michigan. Soon a fierce struggle developed between proponents of gasoline-powered vehicles and supporters of electric or steam-powered devices. The public liked William Morrison's 1891 electric-powered car because of its cleanliness and lack of noise, and they were intrigued by Francis and Freelan Stanley's steam-powered machine. But these ideas soon fell by the wayside because they could not compete with the gasoline-propelled engines for power and speed.

In 1899 Ransom Olds opened his Olds Motor Works in Detroit, where he assembled the first car to be produced in large numbers—the Oldsmobile. While it grabbed the nation's fancy and even became famous in a popular song as the "Merry Oldsmobile," the public still clamored for something faster than the 14-mile-per-hour speed attained by the car.

In the same year, Henry Ford stamped Detroit as the nation's automotive center by starting the Detroit Automobile Company. After experiencing a bumpy beginning and changing the name to the Henry Ford Company, the genius from Dearborn, Michigan, started again in 1903 with the Ford Motor Company.

Other inventors had been streamlining the car with a string of advancements in the early 1900s. The first passenger car with a V-8 engine appeared in 1907, an electric starter replaced the awkward hand cranking device, and aluminum and alloy steels produced lighter, yet more durable, cars.

In 1908 Henry Ford handed the automotive industry its greatest advancement by perfecting the mass production of cars. He was able to increase the yearly output, decrease the cost per car, and maintain high quality by churning out uniform parts. He explained, "The way to make automobiles is to make one automobile like another automobile, to make them all alike, to make them come from the factory just alike—just like one pin is like another pin when it comes from a pin factory." In 1900 automakers sold only 4,192 cars; the number soared in 1908 to 65,000, most of them Ford's famous Model T, known as the "Tin Lizzie." With this accomplishment, supremacy in the automotive industry switched from Europe to the United States.

Every auto manufacturer had to overcome the distrust for these new vehicles by ordinary citizens. Frequent breakdowns and loud noises that emitted from a complicated-appearing engine made the car distasteful to some. One carmaker, Alexander Winton, faced this attitude in the 1890s. When one of his first customers experienced mechanical difficulties, the customer hitched a team of horses to the car and had it pulled through the streets bearing a sign, "This is the only way you can drive a Winton." The carmaker quickly rented a farm wagon, placed a jackass in it, and hired a driver to follow the customer's wagon. Strung out

along the side of Winton's wagon was a sign that stated, "This is the only animal unable to drive a Winton."

Around the same time in Europe, Daimler composed a poem to answer critics who unfavorably compared his car to a horse:

He never eats while in his stall,
Drinks only when he starts to haul,
Plays you no stupid tricks that tease,
Contracts no hoof-and-mouth disease.

Even Henry Ford joined the fray by trying to assure the public that his cars would give customers few problems. An advertisement for his Model A Ford immodestly stated, "It is positively the most perfect machine on the market, having overcome all drawbacks such as smell, noise, jolt, etc., common to all other makes of auto carriages."

Automakers quickly learned that the public could be enticed to purchase their product by staging racing spectacles. Another industry thus arose that captivates audiences to this day—auto racing.

Alexander Winton, an early designer of racing cars, roars around a track in his 1901 speed demon.

3 THE FIRST RACES

"The essence of motor racing is to go as fast as you can without killing yourself," stated auto racer Dan Gurney in the 1960s. His explanation, while simple, pinpointed precisely what racing had entailed since the days when Romans flocked to chariot races—pushing your own talents and your vehicle's limits to achieve maximum performance, yet knowing when to pull back to avoid lying in a mangled heap of twisted metal.

The same spirit moved young American boys to assemble wooden soap box derby racers beginning in the 1930s, and their 1990s counterparts to zoom across parking lots on skateboards and rollerblades.

Speed also fulfilled one of racing's major purposes—to test new vehicles. Racing was the automotive industry's first test track, where engineers determined if the designs they so intricately sketched on paper worked when transformed into metal. As a result, numerous safety devices that modern drivers take for granted first appeared on a race course; improved tires, seat harnesses, and hydraulic disc brakes have saved countless lives.

Automobile racing started in Europe in July 1894 when a French journalist, Pierre Giffard, organized a road test for horseless carriages. Twenty-one vehicles, including seven steam-driven, entered the 78-mile Paris to Rouen competition. Though not actually a race, the event

Drivers line up for the start of a race at the new Indianapolis Speedway in 1909. The Indy 500 began two years later.

Entrants in the 1908 New York to Paris race headed west to the Pacific, where cars and their drivers boarded ships and sailed to Asia, then drove overland to Paris. The survivors arrived several months after they started. Here one entry, loaded down with supplies, pauses in a small town in Iowa.

illustrated the impact such contests would have on automobiles when the steam engines performed poorly. The public quickly turned from steam-operated cars in favor of gasoline-powered automobiles.

The first organized automobile race occurred the following year, when a round-trip Paris to Bordeaux race drew 22 entrants, including 15 gas-propelled, six steam-powered, and one electric-powered vehicle. Nine cars completed the race under the maximum time allotment of 100 hours, led by Emile Levassor's Panhard, which averaged 15 miles per hour for the 732 miles. As with the previous year's event, gasoline-driven cars so outperformed their rivals that their production substantially increased.

Town-to-town road races, which sent out the contestants at one-minute intervals and then timed their performances, dominated the sport in these early years. A Paris-Amsterdam-Paris race took place in 1898; a Paris-Vienna spectacle in 1902 wound the contestants through the challenging Alps. Dozens of such races dotted Europe in the 1890s and 1900s. A 1,000-mile London-Edinburgh-London road race in 1900 coursed through many of Great Britain's major cities and illiustrated for an admiring nation the durability of these new machines. Interest and sales in automobiles boomed in England following the event.

Most amazing of the long-distance races may have been the 10,000-mile 1907 Peking to Paris road race, won by the Italian Scipio Borghese in a 1907 Itala vehicle. Though road maps had not come into use and no one had ever driven from China to Paris, Borghese drove through China, the Gobi Desert, Siberia, Moscow, St. Petersburg, Berlin, Amsterdam, and Brussels, and reached Paris after two months. The second-place driver arrived three weeks later.

There was nothing normal about this race. Rival drivers agreed to assist each other in case of accidents along the way, and frequent detours had to be taken to avoid lakes, streams, impassable terrain, and weather. Borghese faced heat and cold, rain, mud, bugs, quicksand, swamps, deserts, and cliffs. Three times his car caught fire because of overheated brakes. Whenever the car quit or a part broke, he had to be imaginative in finding a solution. One time his rear wheel collapsed near a tiny Siberian village. Borghese located the village blacksmith, and although he had never seen a car before, the blacksmith used an ax to cut wood for wooden spokes and a red hot poker to make bolt holes.

Borghese hired teams of oxen, horses, and men to pull his car through mud and swamps or over cliffs and hills. A journalist who accompanied Borghese wrote about heading into a swampy area. "The soil under our feet was heaving. It was as if we were walking over floating cork. We realized that the mass of mud would swallow up our car if we did not succeed in saving it at once."

Borghese hooked the car to a team of oxen, but the animals had trouble freeing the vehicle from the suction. Borghese jumped into the car and started the engine, which he knew would cause a startling backfire. The noise so scared the oxen that they lurched forward and pulled the car out.

The 1908 New York-to-Paris race proved to be the premier long-distance event. After leaving New York on February 12, contestants crossed the United States, then boarded a freighter for the lengthy Pacific Ocean trip to the city of Vladivostok on Russia's eastern coast. They drove across Asia into Europe and finally on to Paris. Cars from four different nations entered the event, which was won by an American who crossed the finish line on July 30.

The Gordon Bennett Races tried to bring Europe's capitals closer together in terms of travel time and sportsmanship. Named after an American newspaperman, this series of

city-to-city contests lasted less than two years as entrants spent too much time arguing over rules.

Though road races brought publicity to the industry and helped to sell cars, they were too dangerous to be held for long. Spectators, unaware of the danger they faced, lined both sides of the road to get a glimpse of the speeding vehicles. Any car that spun out of control would bounce directly into the crowd. In 1901 a racer accidentally killed a boy who had wandered onto the road during the Paris-Berlin race, and two years later a major disaster in France forced the government to halt such exhibitions.

Accidents marred the race from the start. A newspaper reporter wrote that, "The most

In Europe, racers braved gravel roads through mountain passes. Early auto designer Vincenzo Lancia maneuvers a 1908 Fiat around a mountain curve in a race in Italy.

terrible sight of all was the wreck of Lorraine Barrow's car. It was the most complete wreck ever known. When doing over 80 mph he struck a dog. A child dashed out and a soldier rushed to save it. The body of the dog had jammed the steering, with the result that both soldier and child were run down and killed and the car went end-on into a tree." The car, with its driver, disintegrated and showered the surrounding crowd with sharp metal parts. To prevent other incidents, the French government halted races between cities.

In 1906 the first Grand Prix was staged near Le Mans, France. Rather than dashing from city to city, cars navigated a 23-mile course that wound through the French countryside and ended where it started. In this historic Grand Prix, the winning driver succeeded mainly because his car, a French Renault, carried an innovation his competitors did not have—detachable rims. Since frequent tire changes were the norm in those days, he and his mechanic were able to quickly unbolt the flat or damaged tire and replace it with a new one, whereas the other drivers had to pry the tires off the old-style rims.

To get additional power, engineers simply made larger engines. In 1907, the rules placed a limit on the amount of fuel a car could use and severely restricted engine sizes in hopes of encouraging automakers to develop an improved product. Classes, called formulas, were put into the Grand Prix events to separate different sizes of cars.

More efficient and faster cars resulted, beginning with a French car, the Peugeot, which entered the 1912 Grand Prix. Containing an engine barely half the size of the other racers, the Peugeot also sported four-wheel brakes, knock-off wheels, and a streamlined body for better aerodynamics instead of the larger, block-type frame. The Peugeot easily won the race and ended the dominance of large cars and bulky engines. Designers and racers from every other automotive company put their efforts into copying what Peugeot had done.

Not every improvement originated in Europe. Across the Atlantic, a growing circle of American sportsmen and car enthusiasts were busily putting their ingenuity to the wheel.

4 FASTER, FASTER, FASTER

Though Europeans started auto racing, similar developments unfolded across the Atlantic Ocean. Frank Duryea captured the first race in the United States when he averaged five miles per hour over a 55-mile course to beat five other cars in the *Chicago Times-Herald* event on November 28, 1895. Narragansett Park in Cranston, Rhode Island, opened the first race track the next year, hosting two electric automobiles and two gas-combustion vehicles in one-mile heats. The winner posted a top speed of 26.8 miles per hour.

In 1904 the first Vanderbilt Cup race was staged amidst great controversy on Long Island, New York. Organizers hoped to rival the European road races and encourage American car development, but they only succeeded in gathering opposition. Many Long Island residents protested the use of public roads as dangerous and inconvenient, and homeowners carefully watched practice runs to record the number of any racing car that exceeded the legal speed limit.

However, the race took place as planned, with top speeds that thrilled the spectators who lined the streets along the 30-mile course. To the racers zooming by, though, the race was much different from what the fans noticed. One driver explained, "The people just seem to be a black and white border to the dark street in front. Yes, you hear them shout, but by the time you realize it, you are gone. If you're used to

The Vanderbilt Cup race over public roads on Long Island was the blue ribbon event of American auto racing in the first decade of the 20th century. Men climbed telephone poles to get a better view.

racing, you don't think about dangers. You'd go ahead even if you know there was a precipice ahead. All you want is to go faster, faster, faster. You can't go fast enough for the man who likes to race. Never! Speed mania they call it. Ah, but it's fine, fine!"

Reaction to the race, won by George Heath in a Panhard car, was far from enthusiastic. One writer for the *New York Times* declared the race "not as exciting as a horse race. For long stretches of time, there was nothing to be seen. Then, there would be a megaphoned yell of 'car coming' and a gray, blue, or white streak would shoot by with a deafening noise, and all would be over." Another observer grumped, "It was all very fine, but the automobile will never take the place of the horse for sporting men."

While European racing focused mainly on city-to-city races or courses that wound through the countryside, American racing gradually settled on dirt tracks and oval courses. Developers constructed a wooden-board oval speedway with banked sides in Los Angeles in 1910, a design that was quickly duplicated at

Legendary racer Barney Oldfield poses in his favorite car, the 999 Ford built for him by Henry Ford, standing beside him.

numerous locations around the nation. Drivers staged daredevil speed races to thrill the audience. Races were often rigged so that the crowd's favorite racer could rush across the finish line at the last moment. Eventually, the American Automobile Association began supervising these events, eliminating the staged spectacles in favor of actual races.

Drivers faced known and unknown hazards. Cars broke down and endangered all participants; they rolled over or became airborne with alarming regularity; and few safety precautions had yet been adopted for the drivers' welfare. The wooden boards that composed the race track often loosened as the race wore on, sometimes even causing cars to break through. One driver, Wilbur Shaw, recalled a race where young kids crept out of the stands, sneaked under the wooden track, and poked their heads up through holes in the track. Shaw's heart practically stopped when he turned a corner and spotted small heads sticking up through the track. He and his opponents had to swerve out of the way to avoid running over the foolish youngsters.

One Florida dirt track in Daytona Beach became a favorite of many racers. The first race held at the site, in 1902, pitted Ransom Olds against Alexander Winton. When each hit a top speed of 57 miles per hour, the two declared the race a tie. The next year Winton became the first driver to shatter the mile-a-minute barrier when he posted a 68.19 mark in winning another event at Daytona Beach.

This seemed the signal for an onslaught of attempts to smash the one-mile speed record. First set in 1898 when the French racer

Chasseloup-Laubat recorded 39.2 miles per hour, the mark quickly soared. Henry Ford pushed one of his cars to 90 mph in 1904, and Barney Oldfield, who was to become a legend in auto racing for Ford, rocketed to 131 mph in 1910.

At about the same time, a track opened in the Midwest. The 2.5-mile Indianapolis course, consisting of a limestone and gravel surface and bordered by three miles of whitewashed fence, at first was used to test automobile improvements. However, racing came to the fore, and from it evolved the spectacular competition known as the Indianapolis 500.

The first race, a short-distance affair between huge box-shaped cars resting on wooden-spoked wheels, occurred in 1909. Open cockpits offered little shelter to the racers and the mechanics who rode at their side. A newspaper reporter warned in an article titled "The Return from Death at 60 mph" that driving at such high speeds would result in hearing loss. While incorrect about the hearing, the reporter's foreboding about the race materialized when dust and gravel kicked up from the track blinded many of the participants. After three drivers and two spectators died in the fiasco, the track was resurfaced with brick to avoid similar mishaps.

Personalities dominated the auto racing field in the early days. After organizing the Winton Motor Carriage Company in Cleveland in 1897, Alexander Winton began entering his cars in races held at local horse tracks, where he recorded a top speed of 33 mph. Three years later the legendary Henry Ford defeated Winton, then left the field of racing to focus on auto development. In 1905 H. L. Bowden broke the 100-mph mark at Daytona Beach with a speed of 109.75.

The flamboyant driver Barney Oldfield garnered most of the headlines in the first two decades of the 1900s. In 1910 he hit the then-astounding speed of 131 mph in a race, which he later compared to "the sensation of riding a rocket through space." As daring as Oldfield was, he did not think men would attain much higher speeds. "A speed of 131 mph is as near to the absolute limit of speed as humanity will ever travel," he declared.

Oldfield toured the country to race at county fairs and exhibitions. In one of the most publicized duels of 1917, he squared off in a series of six races against another top-caliber driver, Ralph DePalma, who was as calm and dignified as Oldfield was brash and arrogant. Before the first race Oldfield claimed, "I have been waiting a long time to get DePalma on a dirt track. I'll show him what racing is all about." DePalma answered with typical restraint, "Modesty is a word Greek to Oldfield and he probably has been telling everybody how he is hoping to make me eat his dust."

Oldfield climbed in his car and handily defeated DePalma in the initial match, although he could not resist the temptation to add drama to the affair. According to a reporter who covered the event, "Oldfield's well-known love of the spectacular made a close finish for what was otherwise a one-sided race. He simply slowed up on the final mile, until DePalma was almost abreast of him. At that point, Oldfield put his foot on it. He beat Ralph down the stretch and across the finish line by a foot or two. It was a sensational finish and gave the crowd a thrill."

The pair, who actually respected each other's talents, staged the other five events in different parts of the country. Oldfield, true to his brash words, won four of the six races.

However, DePalma, who was known as "The King of the Roaring Road" because of the many victories he compiled between 1912 and 1930, was beloved as much for his sportsmanship as for his astounding talent behind the wheel.

In one race a local youth broke his arm trying to crank-start DePalma's car. Though he was immersed in pre-race preparations, DePalma drove the young boy to a hospital, hurried back for the race, won his event, then returned to check on the boy. DePalma paid for the entire cost of medical care. In another race featuring a razor-close finish, DePalma informed the judges that his opponent had won by inches, even though the judges had at first declared DePalma the winner.

In the 1912 Milwaukee Grand Prix, Caleb Bragg brushed DePalma's car and knocked it out of control. More than one fistfight has broken out in similar circumstances, but as DePalma was being lifted into an ambulance, he told reporters, "Tell the people Caleb Bragg wasn't to blame, boys. He gave me all the road."

Another manner of drawing the nation's attention to the fledgling auto industry was to show that the car could endure the hazards presented by the country's poor road system. Auto producers hoped to illustrate this with long-distance races, which required the vehicles to navigate various terrains and endure the entire spectrum of weather. In

1903 Alexander Winton embarked upon a drive from San Francisco to New York. Observers, figuring that poor roads, weather, and constant mechanical difficulties would impede Winton, predicted the feat might take as much as six months. However, Winton drove into New York City only 63 days after leaving the West Coast. Later that year a second driver, Dr. H. Jackson, duplicated Winton's achievement, even though at one location along his route, Jackson was given a fine for exceeding the six-mph speed limit.

While these races, from county fairs to continent-traversing exhibitions, brought publicity to the automotive industry and proved the car's value to people, they were merely the forerunners of the grand racing spectacles that would astonish the world. One, a series known as the Grand Prix races, blossomed in the 1920s.

Captain Eddie Rickenbacker was a leading auto racer before becoming America's leading air ace in World War I by shooting down 22 enemy planes and 4 balloons. After the war he owned the Indianapolis Speedway for 18 years. Here he poses in his WWI fighter plane. At 52, during WWII, he was in a plane that was forced down in the Pacific Ocean. He and seven others drifted on rubber rafts for 24 days before they were rescued.

5 DRIVING AS AN ART FORM

The exciting races that thrilled Europeans from the early 1900s to 1920 took on an organized format during the next two decades. An English businessman, Walter O. Bentley, dreamed of building a car that would not only win races, but would perform quietly enough to appeal to the female market. He turned to a 1923 event in France, the 24-hour endurance race at Le Mans, in hopes of showcasing such a vehicle.

The organizers of Le Mans, who wanted race cars that could also be purchased by the public, enforced strict rules that approximated what everyday motorists had to do. Drivers were required to run to their cars from a starting line, start the cars, then speed off. The cars had to carry weights that represented passengers. Repairs could only be done with tools and materials brought in the car.

After an ingenious mechanic used bubble gum to repair a puncture hole to the gas tank during the race, Bentley's car finished fourth in the 1923 race, then won the event in 1924. Bentley's sales soared.

While Americans crossed the ocean to challenge in their Stutzes and Chryslers, European racing in the 1920s and 1930s mainly became an intense competition among five vehicles—Bugatti, Alfa Romeo, Mercedes, Porsche, and Ferrari. At first the Alfa Romeo and Bugatti dominated, but technological advances, such as smaller, more

Two Bugattis zoom through a town in Ireland during a 1936 race. No. 9 is driven by Arthur Conan Doyle, the creator of Sherlock Holmes.

powerful engines, lighter but more durable metals, and streamlined aerodynamics, brought the other three to the forefront. In addition, European leaders, such as Germany's Adolf Hitler, encouraged their auto manufacturers to design the fastest vehicles so they could bring glory to the nation.

One industrialist who achieved notoriety in these years was Dr. Ferdinand Porsche, whose radical new design thrust his company into competition with the other great German automaker, Mercedes-Benz. Rather than keeping the engine in front of the driver, Porsche switched its location behind the seat. This enabled him to eliminate certain parts that added excess weight. By 1934, employing the maximum amount of lightweight alloy steels, aluminum, amd magnesium, Porsche's cars registered speeds up to 170 mph.

As certain companies monopolized European racing, a select group of talented drivers dominated Grand Prix racing. Foremost were Tazio Nuvolari, Rudolf Caracciola, and Bernd Rosemeyer. A reporter once asked Nuvolari if he thought he would die racing cars. When the driver answered yes, the reporter wondered why he continued to race if he expected death. Nuvolari stared at the man, then asked the reporter if he thought he would die in bed. The reporter replied that he hoped so. "Then I don't know how you get the courage to go to bed every night," stated the driver.

Of the three, Rosemeyer snared the most headlines with his daring style. Caracciola claimed, "Bernd literally did not know fear, and sometimes that is not good. We actually feared for him in every race. Somehow I never

thought a long life was on the cards for him. He was bound to get it sooner or later." Bernd's father once pestered him to quit the dangerous sport, but Bernd replied, "Maybe I too will have to die, but you must understand that without a racing car it is in any case the end of life for me."

The unpredictable Rosemeyer usually jumped into his car like a sheriff vaulting onto his horse. On extremely hot days, he loved to peel off his shirt to get some sun while he drove. After Porsche hired him, every morning Rosemeyer placed a note on his team manager's desk inquiring, "When will that brilliant new driver, Rosemeyer, be allowed to win a race for Auto-Union [Porsche]?"

Bernd Rosemeyer wins the Eiffel race at Nurburgring in 1936.

Though brash, he amazed onlookers with his driving skills. During one race Rosemeyer's brakes locked up as he approached a severe corner. The car skidded, leaped a ditch, and headed directly toward a narrow opening between a stone bridge and a telephone pole. As spectators watched in horror, expecting a shattering collision, Rosemeyer regained control of the car and barely steered it between the obstacles. Afterwards, Dr. Porsche measured the opening through which Rosemeyer guided his car and discovered that it was only one inch wider than Rosemeyer's vehicle.

Bernd Rosemeyer epitomized the best—and the worst—qualities of a race car driver. He feared no race or speed attempt, and while that quality produced a superb handler of cars, it also caused his death. He loved setting speed records in the 10-mile straight runs in Germany. The effort from these ordeals so drained Rosemeyer that he frequently had to remain in his car upon completion until he could regain his strength. As he described it, he faced numerous dangers in these runs.

"The road seemed like a narrow white band, the bridges like tiny black holes ahead. It was a matter of threading the car through them.

"At about 240 mph, the joints in the concrete road surface are felt like blows, setting up a corresponding resonance through the car, but this disappears at a greater speed. Passing under bridges the driver receives a terrific blow to the chest, because the car is pushing air aside, which is trapped by the bridge.

"When you go under a bridge, for a split second the engine noise completely disappears and then returns like a thunderclap when you are through.

"The utmost concentration is needed to keep the car on the road—particularly near the bridges—because side winds are strong and erratic. It is necessary to make tiny, lightning adjustments to the steering all the time, and after a few minutes the driver's nervous energy is completely exhausted.

"The strain of the 10-mile record attempts is actually greater than that of an entire Grand Prix, although the whole thing lasts less than three minutes."

On January 28, 1938, Rosemeyer set up for another 10-mile attempt. The windy day scared off the other racers, and even the great driver Rudolph Caracciola advised Rosemeyer to wait until a calmer day. However, wind and danger meant little to Rosemeyer. He started down the run, but the blustery conditions were too much. He lost control of the car, went sideways off the road, bounced into the air, and crashed in a field. Wreckage was thrown over a 600-yard area. Rosemeyer died doing what he loved best.

Gradually, Grand Prix racing evolved into its current format; smaller, faster cars compete in 19 short-distance Formula One contests, while the wider, heavier Sports Car events are endurance runs such as the 24 Hours of Le Mans and the 1,000 Kilometers of Nurburgring in Germany. In either case, the racing provides more challenge than oval circuits used by American championship and stock cars, since Grand Prix courses wind through city streets and country roads. Grand Prix drivers are constantly shifting gears and negotiating numerous curves and uneven ground.

Before the 1940s, the Grand Prix world champion was the racer who captured the one event considered the Grand Prix of Europe race. Now, a driver receives eight points for winning an event, six points for second place, four for third, three for fourth place, and two points for placing fifth. The driver who records the single fastest lap time during each race also receives one point. The scores for each driver's six best races are added up, and whoever totals the most points is that year's world champion.

Stirling Moss, who along with Mike Hawthorn and Peter Collins formed a famed British trio of drivers labeled the "Three Musketeers" in the 1950s, stated that the exhausting driving demanded by Grand Prix racing requires a true specialist. "I believe that driving, as practiced by some very few people in the world, is an art form, and is related to the ballet. Driving is certainly like ballet in that it is all discipline, rhythm, movement."

Banked wooden tracks built in baseball parks made midget auto racing popular in the 1930s.

Almost 200 different curves await the driver along Nurburgring's 15-mile course, and the pressure mounts when the weather turns ugly.

The importance of teams became more relevant to racing. Besides the driver, each car possessed a squad of mechanics, managers, and other workers who ensured that the vehicle performed at its optimum. With ever-increasing amounts of money available for winning efforts, the amateur drivers of racing's earlier days were replaced by professional racers backed by competent teams.

One of the greatest Grand Prix drivers was the Argentine Juan Fangio, who won five world championships in the 1950s. His performance during the 1957 Nurburgring event in Germany typified what Grand Prix drivers faced. Set in the breathtaking Bavarian Alps and winding by the beautiful 12th-century Schloss Nurburg castle, deadly challenges lay hidden along the lengthy Nurburbring course. Bumpy concrete delivered a hard pounding to the cars, which had to endure continuous twists and turns, rises and dips. To avoid any mishaps, Fangio studied the course until he knew every bump and crack. He memorized the subtleties of each turn and planned where he could shave time and where he should drive with caution.

On August 4, 1957, Fangio climbed into his car. He held back a bit during the first lap, since he wanted to check the surface, but he soon shot into the lead. A confused pit stop of 50 seconds cost Fangio the lead, and the driver roared out of the pit area trailing Mike Hawthorn and Peter Collins by 48 seconds. Figuring that he had to take risks if he was to narrow the gap, Fangio hit each

Juan Fangio of Argentina crosses the finish line of a Paris Grand Prix race in an Alfa Romeo.

curve at what he thought would be the car's maximum speed. Bouncing on the uneven concrete, Fangio's car slid perilously near the course's edge on a number of curves, but still the racer pushed on.

Gradually, he inched closer to his opponents. Fangio and Collins approached one turn almost dead even, but Fangio coaxed a bit more speed out of his car and sped by Collins, kicking up gravel that cracked Collins's goggles and caused him to slow down. Fangio crept toward Hawthorn and, by taking a few more curves at breathtaking speed, took the lead with two laps remaining. After winning the race, Fangio stated, "I did things I've never done before, and I don't ever want to drive like that again." However, Fangio knew his car's limits, pushed it to the edge, and succeeded.

While European auto racing focused on the Grand Prix circuit, racing in America developed along different lines. In addition to the

Indianapolis 500, hundreds of county fairs hosted races at their oval dirt tracks, enabling drivers to enter a race in one location one day, then hasten to another county for a second race the next day. American drivers received more experience in one year hustling from fair to fair than their European counterparts received in a career.

Two of the most successful American drivers in the 1920s and 1930s were Wilbur Shaw and Louis Meyer. Between them they garnered six Indianapolis 500 titles and five national championships. Despite their success, the perils of racing rattled even these performers. On his first race at Indianapolis in 1924, Shaw could not believe the speed at which everyone drove. "I felt I had been sucked into a hundred-mile-an-hour tornado," he exclaimed. "I was never so scared in my life."

While Europeans made most of the headlines in racing before 1940, American drivers dominated afterwards. One of the reasons was the rise of a new form of racing—stock cars.

6

CONQUERING FEAR

"The competition was brutal in those days, though that was before the superspeedways began to dominate things." Driver Tim Flock spoke these words, referring not to the Grand Prix or the Indianapolis 500, but to a distinctively American form of racing—stock cars.

According to legend, stock car racing grew out of the bootlegging days during the 1920s and 1930s, when southern bootleggers (men who made and sold illegal liquor) altered their old cars so that, even with a full load of alcohol, they could outrun state troopers. Driver Curtis Turner claimed he could get his souped-up 1940 Ford to 100 mph on the Virginia back roads. "Some ol' state trooper ran me 39 times, but he never come close. I used to talk with that ol' trooper and he'd say, 'I'm gonna catch you if it's the last thing I do, Curtis.' He never did."

Gradually, men like Turner began to fill idle time by racing against each other. After World War II, when new cars once again rolled off assembly lines, plenty of old cars and spare parts became available. Men started tinkering with the frames and engines, then taking them to local tracks to enter races.

The first race for what were called stock cars—vehicles that were made from auto parts that can be purchased over the counter instead of specially adapted vehicles—occurred at Daytona Beach on March 3, 1936. The 250-mile

Knowing the risks that go with their way of life, auto racers take caution—but not fear—into their cars with them. Safety measures have come a long way since these tiny, open-cockpit midget autos raced on wood and dirt tracks.

event wound down Atlantic Avenue for 1.5 miles, then swerved over the sand dunes and onto the beach where the drivers sped through the surf. Milt Marion finished first and took the $5,000 winner's share.

In that same race, a driver named Bill France placed fifth. However, he made a name in stock car racing not only for his exceptional driving talents, but for organizing a chaotic group of racers and events into what is now one of sport's most popular industries. In 1938 he began managing the Daytona Beach race. His skill at transforming a money-loser into a profitable event drew attention in other circles, and by the mid-1940s he was promoting events in other states.

In 1946 France hoped to stage a 100-mile national championship for stock cars in Charlotte, North Carolina, but another leading figure, Wilton Garrison, told him he could not. "You might call it a North Carolina championship race," explained Garrison, "but you have got to have some kind of a national organization to call it a national championship race."

France formed the National Championship Stock Car Circuit in 1946 and, behind the slogan "WHERE THE FASTEST THAT RUN, RUN THE FASTEST," sanctioned events throughout the country. The following year the organization became known as the National Association for Stock Car Auto Racing (NASCAR), which has operated stock car racing ever since. Today, NASCAR sponsors more than 1,000 events of all sizes, including the most popular circuit, the Grand National.

Under NASCAR's guidance, the sport grew rapidly. The first official race took place at

Daytona Beach on February 14, 1948. Two years later the Darlington Raceway in South Carolina hosted stock car racing's first 500-mile event, which became a staple on the Grand National Circuit. In 1959 the Daytona Speedway opened. It closely resembled Indianapolis but had higher-banked walls so the cars could go faster.

Automakers quickly spotted a profitable market in stock car racing, since the cars closely resembled the current model cars that customers could purchase at their local dealers. They noticed that when a car won an event on Sunday, they could count on increased sales the following week. As a result, Fords, Chevrolets, and Dodges dominated stock car racing. The cars may have looked the same as those in showrooms, but under the hood everything was different, as NASCAR eased restrictions on engine modifications.

What has not changed since racing's earliest days is the caliber of driver. The demanding sport exacts a heavy toll on its participants, and only a few can perform up to its taxing standards. Richard Petty explained, "You've either got it or you don't. You can't train for it, and all the practice in the world won't help if you don't have it. It's not only raw ability, but sort of instinct for knowing when to pass and when to not pass, and when to charge and when to lay back, and just how much your car can take that day in that race on that track. You have to push everything as far as it'll go and if you push any further, forget it."

The men who have succeeded in stock car racing range from the flamboyant Tim Flock, who captured the 1955 NASCAR championship by winning 18 races, to the driving star of the 1990s, Jeff Gordon. Flock later boasted that he would have won 19 races in 1955 had it not been for a monkey named Jocko Flocko that rode with him in races. "I had a seat for Jocko and a seat belt. During a race at Raleigh [North Carolina] he got loose from the seat belt, became frightened, and got on my shoulder and around my neck. I had to stop and put him out. I finished second."

In 1995 Jeff Gordon became the youngest driver to win a NASCAR championship in 50 years. Besides talent and intuition, Gordon performed so well because of his love for speed and his attitude that he could overcome obstacles. He stated that he does not fear

Richard Petty's crew works on his car during a pit stop in the Times 500 NASCAR race in Ontario in 1979. Petty won the Winston Cup NASCAR championship that year.

death as much as being injured and confined to a wheelchair, then immediately hedged even those words. "I think they're [wheelchairs] cool. If I was ever in one I'd have the fastest motorized wheelchair there was."

While drivers are hooked on attaining high speeds, they also battle against a fear of speed. As average speeds in stock car races hit 200 mph, Cale Yarborough muttered, "I don't know how much faster a man can go and still control a car. Sometimes it seems we're hurtling out of control. And it scares you." However, they keep heading back to the track, in spite of the danger, because that is what they do. Another stock car driver, Joe Weatherly, claimed he was scared when he raced, but "you wouldn't want it too safe. What would be the fun of it then?"

The fun came from conquering the fear and, of course, from winning. In auto racing, the ultimate victory—the one that might be called the Super Bowl of racing—remained the Indianapolis 500.

WHY THEY RACE

7

While three major types of racing eclipse all the others—NASCAR's stock car racing, Formula One's Grand Prix events, and CART's Indy Car races such as the Michigan 500—one event overshadows its competitors. Occupying racing's premier position is the Indianapolis 500, held each year on Memorial Day weekend. Since its beginnings in 1911, race car drivers have looked upon it as the ultimate challenge and the race they most want to win.

Former Indy winner Jimmy Bryan declared, "If you never win another dollar in racing the rest of your life, you will still be someone if you have won the Indianapolis 500." Driver Eddie Sachs, who died in a flaming crash during the 1964 Indy 500, so loved the race that he said, "I think of Indianapolis every day of the year, every hour of the day, and when I sleep, too. On the morning of the race, if you told me my house had burned down, I'd say, 'So what?'"

The first Indianapolis race was won by Ray Harroun, who along the way showed that auto racing leads to practical improvements in everyday cars. Harroun, hoping to be aware of what was happening behind his vehicle, rigged a rearview mirror to his car. This item today is taken for granted by drivers, both on and off the race course.

One of the 500's first stars was Wilbur Shaw. Born in Shelbyville, Indiana in 1902, Shaw was fascinated with cars. In his teenage years he

Richard Petty, driving No. 43, is on the guard rail after hitting the wall in a three-car collision at the first turn of Atlanta International Raceway during the Atlanta 500 in 1973.

Forty-seven cars entered the first Indy 500 in 1911, won by Ray Harroun driving a Marmon Wasp.

built a racer on the second floor of a warehouse. To move it to street level he attached a ramp to the building's side. After almost ruining the car while getting it out of the building, Shaw arrived at a track in Lafayette, Indiana, where he proceeded to flip the vehicle and demolish it during the race's first lap.

The energetic young man did not let this mishap slow him down. He became a fixture at area race courses, where he begged anyone to let him have a crack at their cars. His ambition and driving talents eventually earned him the opportunity to race.

Though he first raced in the 1924 Indianapolis 500, where he placed fourth, his 1931 effort is more memorable. On the 60th lap, Shaw attempted to pass another vehicle, but he drove too deeply into a turn, skidded over the wall, vaulted 30 feet, and crashed hard onto the ground. Neither Shaw nor his mechanic was seriously hurt. After being bandaged, Shaw jumped into his team's second car and returned to the track. As he passed other drivers, his opponents almost lost control. They had seen Shaw spin off the track and assumed he was dead, but there he was, like a ghost returned to the competition. Shaw, though he knew he had no chance of winning, gamely kept driving and finished sixth.

In 14 Indy 500 races, the talented Shaw won three times and finished second or third on another four occasions. In the 1941 race, Shaw tried to become the first four-time winner of the event, but a wheel ripped loose on his car, which slammed him into the wall. Although he eventually recovered from his injuries, Shaw never raced again.

Two cars dominated the Indianapolis 500 during the 1920s by winning eight of the 10 races—the Duesenberg and the Miller. Though the race's governing body placed new restrictions on engine size in hopes of containing

Wilbur Shaw in the car he drove to victory in the 1940 Indy 500.

speed, other advancements in body design and weight of metals negated the restrictions. In 1925, Peter de Paolo raced home as the first driver to average 100 mph for the entire race when he registered 101.13. By the 1930s, when drivers started donning sturdy crash helmets instead of the less protective cloth helmets, the average speed zoomed to almost 120 mph.

Large corporations, realizing that the public could be persuaded to purchase products shown on race cars, entered the scene during the 1960s. Sleek, low-lying racers sported company logos touting everything from cigarettes to oil. A victory in an important race, especially the Indy 500, translated into enormous sales for the sponsoring companies. Whereas racing had been a proving ground for adaptations that would benefit the public, racing became a war between companies to win races.

Racing teams arrived in Indianapolis in early May to begin preparing for the race. On the two weekends prior to the race, qualifying trials determined which 33 cars would start. For the entire month, more than one million spectators attended the time trials, practices, and race, with 300,000 packing the stands for the race itself.

Still called "the Brickyard," the 2.5-mile circuit has been paved over, with only a cere-monial strip of bricks crossing the starting line. Otherwise, the track is identical to that used in 1911. However, speeds have risen through the years, until now Indy cars average anywhere from 145 mph to 170 mph. In 1990, Arie Luyendyk set a record when he averaged 185.981 mph in winning the event.

While legendary names like A. J. Foyt, Mario Andretti, Dale Earnhardt, Richard Petty, and

Alain Prost continued to capture racing enthusiasts' fancy, newer personalities entered the
scene in the mid-1990s.

Twenty-four-year-old Jacques Villeneuve,
the son of a Formula One driver who was
killed in a 1982 crash, captured the 1995
Indy 500 with an average speed of 153.616.
The next year he switched to Formula One
driving when he signed a $6 million contract
with the highly-regarded Williams Grand Prix
Engineering team.

Jeff Gordon, 24, quickly rose to the top in
NASCAR events the same year, winning three
of the season's first six races. When he finished
the season with more Winston Cup points
than any other driver, he became the youngest
man to win the NASCAR championship.

Michael Schumacher, 26, won half of his
16 races in 1994 to capture the World Driving
Championship of Formula One racing, then
signed a $24 million contract to drive for
Ferrari. These three young men showed that
racing continued to maintain its vast appeal
for all ages.

Modern racing seems to be more about
glamor or money, but winning and pushing
the car to the limits continues to bring racers
to the tracks. A. J. Foyt said, "The day you're
happy with second or third place is the day
you should get out of racing. I'll make the
same effort if I'm running for a dollar as I will
for $100,000." Fellow driver Parnelli Jones
mentioned that "I really got a big kick out of
every race I ever ran."

Asked why he raced, Mario Andretti said,
"If I stay home one weekend, I become irritable.
I can't help it, but if there's a race in Timbuktu,
I've got to be there. I want to keep driving for

*1994 Winston Cup champ-
ion Dale Earnhardt looks
up at the dark skies after
leaving his car when rain
delayed the running of the
Daytona 500 in 1995.*

as long as I can. I figure I was put on this earth to drive race cars.

"I love race cars and that's why I get involved with so many different types of them. One of the great thrills in my life is being given a new race car that is very sophisticated and making it perform to the utmost of my capabilites.

"It's simple, really. I enjoy racing. I would give up everything—my home, my family, everything I've gained—to stay in racing."

In addition to winning races, drivers have pushed the limits of themselves and their machines in pursuit of speed records. In 1927 an Englishman, H.O.D. Seagrave, became the first to break the 200-mph mark, at Daytona Beach. Ten years later the scene shifted to a smoother track at the Bonneville Salt Flats in Utah.

Aided by the development of more powerful engines, and then jets, drivers rapidly passed the 300, 400, and 500 mph levels. Craig Breedlove, an American driver, set five records along the way.

In 1979 a rocket-powered car driven by stuntman Stan Barrett hit an unofficial speed of 739.6 mph at Edwards Air Force Base, California. No certified timers were present, so his time was not accredited. The official record of 633.468 was set by Richard Noble of England in 1983.

The next challenge for land-based daredevils was to break the sound barrier, which had been achieved in the air by test pilot Chuck Yeager on October 14, 1947. The speed of sound varies on the ground, depending on temperature and altitude. The higher the temperature, the faster it travels. In the desert its normal speed ranges between 750 and 770 mph.

In 1997 Richard Noble led a team that developed the Thrust SSC, a seven-ton car powered by two Rolls-Royce jet engines generating the power of 100,000 horses. They took the black car to Black Rock Desert, Nevada, in September, determined to break the sound barrier. In three runs across the 13-mile course on October 13, Andy Green, a Royal Air Force pilot, set off sonic booms as he zipped through the measured mile at a supersonic 764.168 mph.

In order to qualify for an official speed record, his last two runs had to be completed within 60 minutes. It took 61 minutes to prepare the Thrust for the third run. Despite an average speed of 762 for the last two runs, the official speed record remained the subsonic 714.144 that Green had driven the Thrust on September 25.

Undaunted, Craig Breedlove continued to ready his *Spirit of America* jet car to reclaim the land speed record and became the first to do it in supersonic time.

Man's romance with the automobile, which began when he first replaced the buggy whip with a steering wheel, shows no signs of waning.

CHRONOLOGY

1769	Nicholas Cugnot builds a steam-powered carriage.
1860	Etienne Lenoir develops the first internal-combustion engine.
1885	Karl Benz creates a motorized tricycle.
1891	Emile Levassor creates a motorized buggy.
1893	Charles and Frank Duryea attach a gasoline engine to a carriage.
1894	Paris-Rouen road test occurs.
1895	The first organized race occurs between Paris and Bordeaux, France.
	The first auto race occurs in the United States, the *Chicago Times-Herald* race.
1899	Ransom Olds begins production of his "Merry Oldsmobile".
1902	Daytona Beach hosts its first race.
1903	Henry Ford opens the Ford Motor Company.
	Alexander Winton drives from San Francisco to New York to prove the automobile's durability.
1904	First Vanderbilt Cup race occurs.
1905	H. L. Bowden cracks the 100-mph mark at Daytona Beach.
1906	First Grand Prix takes place near Le Mans, France.
1907	The first passenger car with a V-8 engine appears.
	Peking-Paris road race takes place.
1908	The New York-Paris road race takes place.
	Henry Ford perfects mass production of cars.
1910	A wooden-board oval speedway, the forerunner of thousands to appear throughout the United States, opens in Los Angeles, California.
1911	The first Indianapolis 500 is won by Ray Harroun.
1912	The Peugeot, with its smaller engine, revolutionizes Grand Prix racing.
1920s	Alfa Romeo and Bugatti cars dominate Grand Prix racing.
1925	Peter de Paolo becomes the first driver to average over 100 mph in the Indianapolis 500.
1927	H. O. D. Seagrave breaks the 200-mph barrier at Daytona Beach.
1930s	Porsche monopolizes Grand Prix racing.
1936	First stock car race occurs.

CHRONOLOGY

1938   Bernd Rosemeyer dies in a violent crash.

1947   NASCAR is founded.

1950s   Juan Fangio wins five world championships in Grand Prix racing.

1969   Mario Andretti wins the Indianapolis 500.

1983   Richard Noble sets the land speed record of 633.468 mph.

1990   Arie Luyendyk sets a speed record in the Indianapolis 500 by registering 185.981 mph.

1994   Michael Schumacher signs a 24 million dollar contract with Ferrari.

1995   Jeff Gordon becomes the youngest driver to win a NASCAR championship.

1997   Andy Green clocks the first official supersonic land speed, driving the Thrust SSC 764.168 mph at Black Rock Desert, Nevada.

FURTHER READING

Andretti, Mario with Bob Collins. *What's It Like Out There?*
    Chicago: Henry Regnery Company, 1970.

Gunnell, John A., Editor. *Race Car Flashback.* Iola, Wisconsin:
    Krause Publications, 1994.

Libby, Bill. *Foyt.* New York: Hawthorn Books, Inc., 1974.

————. *Great American Race Drivers.* New York:
    Cowles Book Company, Inc., 1970.

Orr, Frank. *World's Great Race Drivers.* New York: Random House, 1972.

Prentzas, G. S. *Mario Andretti.* New York: Chelsea House Publishers, 1996.

Stevenson, Peter. *The Greatest Days of Racing.* New York:
    Charles Scribner's Sons, 1972.

INDEX

PICTURE CREDITS AP/Wide World: pp. 1, 6, 9, 12, 50, 52, 57; National Archives: pp. 16, 39, 44, 46, 54, 60; Library of Congress: pp. 19, 22, 25, 30, 36, 42, 55; New York Public Library: p. 20, 28; Boston Public Library: pp. 14, 35

JOHN F. WUKOVITS is a teacher and writer from Trenton, Michigan, who specializes in history and biography. His books include biographies of World War II Admiral Clifton Sprague, and Barry Sanders, Vince Lombardi, John Stockton, Jack Nicklaus, Tim Allen, Wyatt Earp, and Butch Cassidy for Chelsea House. A graduate of the University of Notre Dame, Wukovits is the father of three daughters—Amy, Julie, and Karen.